How Do Animal Babies Live?

Faith Hickman Brynie

I Like READING About ANIMALS!

Contents

Words to Know.................... 3

Baby Animals.................... 4

Cheetah.......................... 6

Kingfisher........................ 8

Crocodile........................ 10

Lemur............................ 12

Shark............................ 14

Penguin.......................... 16

Elephant........................ 18

Kangaroo........................ 20

Harp Seal........................ 22

Macaque.......................... 24

Cuckoo.......................... 26

Fox.............................. 28

Learn More

    Books 30

    Web Sites................ 30

    Index 32

Note to Parents and Teachers: The *I Like Reading About Animals!* series supports the National Science Education Standards for K–4 science. The Words to Know section introduces subject-specific vocabulary words for the two different reading levels presented in this book (new reader and fluent reader), including pronunciation and definitions. Early readers may need help with these new words.

Words to Know

New Readers

calf (KAF)—A baby animal, such as a baby cow or elephant.

gosling (GAHZ ling)—A baby goose.

fawn (FAWN)—A baby deer.

herd (HURD)—A group of animals that are all the same kind.

joey (JOH ee)—A baby kangaroo.

pouch (POWCH)—A bag or pocket.

Fluent Readers

colony (KAH luh nee)—A group of animals, such as penguins, that live in the same place.

coral reef (KOR ul REEF)—An underwater ridge made of the bodies of hard-shelled sea animals.

mangrove—A tropical tree that grows in marshes and swamps.

mob—A group of kangaroos.

troop—A group of animals, such as monkeys or macaques.

Baby Animals

All animals have babies. Geese have babies called **goslings**. The parents take good care of them. A baby deer is a **fawn**. The mother keeps a close eye on her fawn.

What happens as baby animals grow?

Some baby animals—such as rabbits—stay with their mother. She cares for them and teaches them for weeks, months, or even years.

Other baby animals are on their own from the time they are born. They are born knowing how to find food and shelter and how to find others of their kind.

Let's learn about the lives of some baby animals.

Is this baby animal a kitten?

No. This is a baby cheetah. It is called a cub. It is only two weeks old. When it grows up, it will run fast. ▷

How do adult and baby cheetahs move?

Adult cheetahs are the fastest land animals. They can run as fast as 70 miles (113 kilometers) an hour. Baby cheetahs are not ready to run that fast yet.

This mother cheetah is moving her cub the easy way. She lifts it by the loose skin on its neck. She cares for it until it is old enough to run and hunt on its own.

What are these birds doing?

Baby birds are chicks. These chicks are five days old. They are kingfishers. Their father feeds them fish. The babies will grow up to look like him.

How do babies let their parents know what they need?

These baby kingfishers are two weeks old. They are safe in their underground nest. The parent birds dug the nest into a river bank.

The baby birds need their parents to feed them. The chicks are small, but they are noisy. They call for their parents. It means, "I am hungry. Feed me." They will not leave the nest until they are four weeks old.

Is this baby crocodile safe?

Baby crocodiles come out of eggs. *C-RRR-AAA-CK!*
That shell is hard to break. This baby gets help from
its mother's teeth. ▶

How do mother crocodiles care for their babies?

A female Nile crocodile digs a hole in the bank of the river. She lays between 25 and 100 eggs in her nest. She covers the eggs with sand and guards the nest for three months.

When the eggs are ready to hatch, the babies chirp. Their mother hears them, digs up the eggs, and helps the babies hatch. Then she carries them in her mouth to the water. She watches over them for another two months.

What baby animal is this?

◀ This baby is a crowned lemur (LEE mur). It looks like a monkey, but it is not one. It is only a few days old. It rides on its mother. It stays safe and warm with her.

Where do lemurs live? What do lemurs eat?

The crowned lemur lives in the rainforest on an island off the coast of Africa. This animal lives nowhere else in the world.

Adult crowned lemurs eat mostly fruit. Sometimes they eat leaves, flowers, or insects. A baby lemur can't eat those foods. For the first five or six months of its life, a baby lemur lives on its mother's milk.

Will this mother shark help her baby grow?

This is a lemon shark mother. Her baby is beside her. It was born in water that is not very deep. It will stay there for about seven years. It will grow without any help from its mother. ▶

Where do lemon sharks live? How do they grow?

Lemon sharks grow up in shallow, warm waters close to shore. They often live near coral reefs or mangrove swamps. They eat fish, crabs, and crayfish.

This baby shark will eat and grow for six or seven years. It will be seven feet (more than two meters) long when it is an adult. Then it will swim out into the deeper ocean water.

Is a penguin sitting on this chick?

This chick is a baby emperor penguin. It lives where the weather is cold. The chick sits on a parent's feet. The parent keeps the chick warm and safe.

Where do emperor penguin babies grow up?

Emperor penguins live in Antarctica. They raise their young in large groups, called colonies.

In May, the mother lays one egg. The father tucks the egg into his brood pouch. This pouch is a flap of skin on his belly. The pouch keeps the egg warm for about nine weeks.

After the chick hatches, it stays on the feet of a parent. Its parents take turns finding food for it. In December, all the young penguins are old enough to swim in the ocean and find food for themselves.

What are this mother and baby?

These are African elephants. The baby is called a **calf**. ▷
It stays close to its mother. Elephants live in groups.
The groups are called **herds**.

How do African elephants grow and live?

African elephants are the heaviest of all land animals. This baby weighed about 220 pounds (100 kilograms) when it was born. It will weigh 10,000 pounds (4,500 kilograms) when it is ten years old.

Elephants eat leaves, roots, bark, grasses, and fruit. Females stay with their herds all their lives. Males leave the herd when they are grown.

What animal is hiding here?

This is a baby kangaroo. It is a called a **joey**. The mother kangaroo has a **pouch**. The joey stays in the pouch. It drinks milk there. It will grow in the pouch for almost a year.

How do joeys grow and live?

A joey is less than one inch long at birth. It crawls up the fur on its mother's belly and into her pouch. It drinks her milk for 11 months before it comes out to hop around on its own.

Kangaroos live in family groups called mobs. This joey's mob lives on the grasslands of Australia.

What baby animal is this?

This baby harp seal is called a pup. It was born on the Arctic ice. Its thick fur keeps it warm. It will live in the ocean. ▶

How do harp seals live?

Harp seal pups are born on ice, but they do not stay there long. The pup drinks its mother's milk for only twelve days. The pup gains weight quickly during that time.

During the next ten days, it loses its baby hair and grows a thick fur coat. Then it heads for the water.

Harp seals are fast, strong swimmers. They can dive deep. They eat fish and crabs.

What is this animal doing?

◀ This is a baby Japanese macaque (muh KAK). The mother holds her baby. She keeps it warm and safe. She will teach it many things. She will care for it for two years.

How do macaque babies grow up?

Japanese macaques live in groups called troops. There are usually 20 to 30 animals in a troop. Each troop has an adult male leader. Female macaques stay with the same troop for life. As adults, male macaques will leave to join other troops.

Macaque mothers feed their babies milk. They carry them and protect them from harm. The males in the troop help, too. They carry, snuggle, clean, and protect the babies.

What kind of chick is this?

This chick is a cuckoo. It is in the nest of a different kind of bird! A mother cuckoo laid her egg there. Her chick will be fed by a different mother bird. ▷

Are cuckoos lazy parents?

Cuckoos lay eggs in the nests of reed warblers. Adult warblers naturally feed the biggest open mouth in the nest. When a cuckoo hatches in a warbler nest, it has the biggest mouth. It gets fed. The warbler hatchlings do not.

In this picture, the small bird is the reed warbler parent. It is feeding the big cuckoo chick. The cuckoo parent has tricked a warbler into caring for its chick.

Where are these animals living?

This mother red fox has five babies. They are called cubs or kits. They stay in their home under the ground. The father brings food to the mother.

What do fox cubs learn from their parents?

Fox cubs are born in the spring. They drink milk from their mother's body, and they grow. They stay underground in a den with their mothers until they are four or five weeks old.

Then they can leave the den. All summer long, their parents teach the cubs how to hunt for food. In the fall, the cubs are ready to find hunting grounds of their own.

Learn More

Books

Hewett, Joan. *A Penguin Chick Grows Up*. Minneapolis: Carolrhoda, 2004.

Hickman, Pamela. *Animals and Their Young: How Animals Produce and Care for Their Babies*. Toronto, Ontario: Kids Can Press, 2003.

Maze, Stephanie, ed. *Tender Moments in the Wild: Animals and Their Babies*. Potomac, Md.: Moonstone, 2006.

Simon, Seymour. *Baby Animals*. New York: SeaStar, 2002.

Web Sites

Enchanted Learning.
http://www.enchantedlearning.com/subjects/animals/animalbabies.shtml

National Geographic Kids.
http://kids.nationalgeographic.com/animals

Yahoo Kids. *Kids Study Animals*.
http://kids.yahoo.com/animals

Index

A

Africa, 13, 18
African elephant, 18
Antarctica, 17
Arctic ice, 22
Australia, 21

B

brood pouch, 17

C

calf, 18
cheetah, 6
chick, 9, 17, 26
colony, 17
coral reef, 14
crocodile, 10
crowned lemur, 13
cub, 6, 29
cuckoo, 26

D

den, 29

E

eggs, 10, 17, 26
emperor penguin, 17

F

father, 9, 17, 29
fawn, 5
food, 5, 13, 14, 17, 18, 22, 29

G

gosling, 5

H

harp seal, 22
herd, 18
hunt, 6, 29

J

Japanese macaque, 25
joey, 21

K

kangaroo, 21
kingfisher, 9
kit, 29

L

lemon shark, 14

M

mangrove swamp, 14
milk, 13, 21, 22, 25, 29
mob, 21
mother, 5, 6, 10, 13, 14, 17,
    21, 22, 25, 26, 29

N

nest, 9, 10, 26

P

pouch, 17, 21
pup, 22

R

rabbit, 5
red fox, 29
reed warbler, 26

T

troop, 25

Library of Congress Cataloging-in-Publication Data

Brynie, Faith Hickman, 1946–

    How do animal babies live? / Faith Hickman Brynie.

      p. cm. — (I like reading about animals!)

    Includes bibliographical references and index.

    Summary: "Leveled reader that explains how different animal babies live and grow up in both first grade text and third grade text"—Provided by publisher.

    ISBN 978-0-7660-3327-6

    1. Animals—Infancy—Juvenile literature. 2. Parental behavior in animals—Juvenile literature. I. Title.

QL763.B67 2010

591.3'9—dc22

                2008050056

ISBN-13: 978-0-7660-3748-9 (paperback ed.)

Printed in the United States of America

112009 Lake Book Manufacturing, Inc., Melrose Park, IL

10 9 8 7 6 5 4 3 2 1

To Our Readers: We have done our best to make sure all Internet addresses in this book were active and appropriate when we went to press. However, the author and the publisher have no control over and assume no liability for the material available on those Internet sites or on other Web sites they may link to. Any comments or suggestions can be sent by e-mail to comments@enslow.com or to the address on the back cover.

Photo Credits: Photos by naturepl.com: © Aflo, p. 23; © Andrew Cooper, p. 28; © Angelo Gandolfi, pp. 8, 9; © Anup Shah, pp. 10, 11; © Dave Bevan, p. 4 (inset); © Dave Watts, p. 20; © David Kjaer, p. 26; © Doug Allan, p. 16; © Doug Perrine, pp. 14, 15; © John Cancalosi, p. 27; © Jurgen Freund, p. 22; © Ingo Arndt, pp. 21, 24, 25; © Laurent Geslin, p. 18; © Lynn M. Stone, p. 5; © Pete Oxford, pp. 12, 13, 17; © Rod Williams, p. 4; © Suzi Eszterhas, pp. 6, 7; © T.J. Rich, p. 29; © Tony Heald, p. 19; Yukihiro Fukuda, p. 1. **Photo by Shutterstock**, pp. 2–3, 30–31, 32.

Cover Photo: © Yukihiro Fukuda/naturepl.com

Series Science Consultant:
Helen Hess, PhD
Professor of Biology
College of the Atlantic
Bar Harbor, ME

Series Literacy Consultant:
Allan A. De Fina, PhD
Dean, College of Education/Professor of Literacy Education
New Jersey City University
Past President of the New Jersey Reading Association

Enslow Elementary

an imprint of

Enslow Publishers, Inc.

40 Industrial Road
Box 398
Berkeley Heights, NJ 07922
USA

http://www.enslow.com